Who Was
Jacques Cousteau?

Who Was Jacques Cousteau?

by Nico Medina

illustrated by Dede Putra

Penguin Workshop

For Papa, for instructing me *not*
to chase the barracuda—NM

For my one and only, thank you for the patience
and support—DP

PENGUIN WORKSHOP
An Imprint of Penguin Random House LLC, New York

Text copyright © 2015 by Nico Medina.
Illustrations copyright © 2015 by Penguin Random House LLC. All rights reserved.
Published by Penguin Workshop, an imprint of Penguin Random House LLC, New York.
PENGUIN and PENGUIN WORKSHOP are trademarks of Penguin Books Ltd.
WHO HQ & Design is a registered trademark of Penguin Random House LLC.
Manufactured in China.

Visit us online at www.penguinrandomhouse.com.

Library of Congress Control Number: 2015939753

ISBN 9780448482347   10 9 8 7 6 5 4 3 2

Part of the *What Is Science & Technology?* Boxed Set, ISBN 9780593090138

Contents

Who Was
Jacques Cousteau?

In 1920, ten-year-old Jacques Cousteau and his family were living in New York City.

Jacques and his older brother, Pierre-Antoine, liked playing stickball in the street outside their apartment on West Ninety-Fifth Street.

But besides stickball, Jacques was not a sports fan. He was skinny and sickly, and shy around other kids. Pierre-Antoine was his best friend.

That summer, the brothers were sent away to camp in Vermont. One day, while horseback riding, Jacques's horse threw him to the ground. Jacques refused to ride for the rest of the summer.

Jacques was sent to the lake and ordered to remove leaves and branches from the water so the other boys could have a clean swimming space.

This so-called "punishment" would change Jacques's life forever.

Jacques dived to the bottom of the lake and opened his eyes, hoping to see the underwater world around him. But the water was too muddy. It stung his eyes, and he could barely see past his own two hands.

Regardless, Jacques wanted to linger beneath the surface. He held his breath for as long as he could.

He even tried breathing through a hollow reed (a long, sturdy piece of grass), but that didn't work very well.

Jacques felt free swimming in the water. He welcomed the opportunity to visit the lake every day that summer.

As an adult, Jacques pioneered new techniques for diving, breathing, filming, and even *living* underwater. He outgrew his shyness to become a worldwide celebrity, best-selling author, Oscar-winning moviemaker, and television star who brought breathtaking images of ocean life to millions of people the world over.

Chapter 1
On the Move

On June 11, 1910, in a small French market town fifty miles from the Atlantic coast, Jacques Cousteau was born. (Say his name like this: ZHOCK koo-STOW.) Soon after, Jacques's parents, Daniel and Elizabeth, and older brother, Pierre-Antoine, returned to their home in Paris.

Daniel was an attorney and personal assistant to an American millionaire living there. His job required him to travel with his boss constantly. The Cousteaus were on the move for much of Jacques's early years. One of his first childhood memories was being rocked to sleep on a train.

Although Jacques was weak and often ill, he was determined. On a family trip to Deauville, a fashionable seaside resort, Jacques learned to swim. He was only four.

When World War I broke out in 1914, German soldiers invaded France. Daniel's boss returned to America. Jacques's father was out of a job.

German forces surrounded the city. But the Parisians—with help from their British allies— fought back. Hundreds of taxicabs drove back and forth between the city and the front lines, delivering soldiers and supplies.

The French government left Paris, moving France's capital to the city of Bordeaux. The Germans never conquered Paris, but life in the city was difficult as the war raged on.

Food, water, and electricity were rationed—people were allowed only a certain amount of each resource. German aircraft, called *zeppelins*, dropped bombs on the city.

ZEPPELINS

NAMED FOR THEIR INVENTOR, COUNT FERDINAND VON ZEPPELIN, THESE ENORMOUS AIRSHIPS WERE HUNDREDS OF FEET LONG. THEY FLEW HIGHER THAN MOST PLANES AT THE TIME. RESEMBLING LARGE BLIMPS, THEY WERE MADE OF HARD STEEL SKELETONS COVERED WITH FABRIC, WITH BAGS OF GAS INSIDE THE SKELETONS PROVIDING LIFT, AND ENGINES OUTSIDE THRUSTING THE SHIP FORWARD.

ZEPPELINS BOMBED LONDON AND PARIS THROUGHOUT WORLD WAR I. ALTHOUGH THEIR AIM WAS POOR, THEY COULD DROP MANY BOMBS IN A SHORT AMOUNT OF TIME.

AFTER THE WAR ENDED, ZEPPELINS WERE USED LIKE THE COMMERCIAL AIRPLANES OF TODAY, FLYING PEOPLE BACK AND FORTH ACROSS THE ATLANTIC. IN 1937, WHEN THE FIERY EXPLOSION OF THE *HINDENBURG* AIRSHIP IN NEW JERSEY KILLED THIRTY-SIX PEOPLE, THE AGE OF THE AIRSHIP QUICKLY CAME TO AN END.

When Jacques was seven, he and his family moved back to their village.

In the spring of 1918, the Germans made one final push toward Paris. This time, the Americans were there to help the French and the British. The Germans were pushed back once again. By the end of the year, a cease-fire was called. In 1919, the war formally ended.

After the war, Daniel got a job working for another American millionaire, Eugene Higgins. In 1920, the Cousteaus moved to New York City with Mr. Higgins. On the eight-day voyage across the Atlantic, ten-year-old Jacques began to come out of his shell.

He made friends with the crew, and explored every corner of the huge ship.

In America, Jacques's brother was his only real friend. Pierre-Antoine liked to be called "PAC," the three initials of his name. Jacques decided, to be just like his older brother, he would be called "Jack." It sounded very American.

Jacques did not like school or sports. He liked to build things—like model planes and boats. And he liked to take them apart to see how they worked.

That first summer, Jacques and his brother went to camp in Vermont. That's where Jacques first began to imagine what it would be like to move and breathe freely underwater.

In 1923, the Cousteaus moved back to France. Jacques saved three months' allowance and bought a used Pathé Baby, a hand-cranked movie camera. As soon as Jacques got home, he took the camera apart and put it back together again.

With a camera in his hand, Jacques finally shook off his shyness. Looking through the lens, he could talk to anyone . . . even pretty girls. Jacques made friends, and they made short movies together. At fourteen, Jacques filmed his first full-length feature: a cousin's wedding.

Jacques still disliked school. His grades were bad, and he was more interested in making movies than sitting quietly in a classroom. When he was caught breaking windows in one of the school's stairwells, Jacques said he was only conducting an experiment. He was testing the difference between a rock that was thrown weakly and one that was thrown forcefully.

Jacques conducted this "experiment" on *seventeen windows*! He was expelled from school.

Jacques's parents took away his camera and sent him to a strict boarding school 250 miles away. Strangely, the school's harsh rules suited Jacques, and without his camera to distract him, he blossomed. In 1929, nineteen-year-old Jacques graduated from high school. The next year, he joined the French Navy.

With his trusty camera back in hand, Jacques Cousteau was ready for a life of adventure.

Chapter 2
Shattered Dreams

The navy trained Jacques to be a gunnery officer. That meant he was in charge of the weapons on battleships. After graduating with honors, Jacques spent a year aboard a navy ship with his fellow cadets. They circled the globe, touring the world. This was a requirement of the French Navy—and an exciting one at that!

From pearl divers in the South Pacific to the shores of Japan, Jacques recorded everything with his camera. He even met some Hollywood movie stars while docked in California. After returning to France, he edited his footage and showed it to his family and friends.

But Jacques didn't stay home for long. In 1933, the navy sent him back to the Far East. While on a visit to Japan, Jacques met a French businessman named Henri Melchior. Mr. Melchior ran a company called Air Liquide. It produced and sold compressed air.

Compressed air is air that has been condensed (or pushed together) and stored in a container under high pressure. In the real world, air moves about freely. But when pressure is applied, a large amount of air can be pushed into a small can or a tank.

L'AIR LIQUIDE

Jacques thought that perhaps one day, Mr. Melchior's compressed air could be used to breathe underwater. It would work better than a hollow reed!

Mr. Melchior's daughter, seventeen-year-old Simone, had been raised in the south of France and Japan. She was fluent in both French and Japanese. Her grandfathers and great-grandfather had all been admirals in the navy. She longed for a life at sea full of

SIMONE MELCHIOR

adventure. She and Jacques barely spoke when they first met, but they would meet again soon.

When Jacques returned to France, he requested a transfer to the Naval Aviation Corps. He wanted to become a pilot.

Jacques loved to fly. He took photos of the earth from high in the sky. After six months he had nearly finished his coursework and training.

Then something terrible happened one rainy night in 1936. Jacques borrowed his father's zippy sports car to attend a friend's wedding in the mountains. While approaching a bend in the twisting mountain road, the car's headlights went out.

Jacques crashed into a ditch. Luckily there were no other cars on the road, or Jacques might have been hit. But this also meant there was no one to stop and help him.

Jacques thought he was going to die. Walking and crawling through the pain, he found his way to a nearby house. When he finally reached a hospital, the doctors told him his arm had been shattered. Bones were broken in multiple places, and one of

his arms was badly infected. The doctors wanted to cut off Jacques's arm to stop the spread of infection.

But Jacques refused, saying he would rather die than not have both of his arms.

Amazingly, after months of painful physical therapy, Jacques showed real progress. But one of his arms remained twisted for the rest of his life.

Jacques's dreams of becoming a pilot were over.

Chapter 3
The Sea Musketeers

For months, twenty-six-year-old Jacques stayed with family in Paris and recovered from the accident. One night, he attended a fancy party at Henri Melchior's apartment. With his camera rolling, he spotted a beautiful blond woman across the dance floor. It was Simone. Jacques and Simone ended up talking for hours that night. They were enchanted with each other.

When the navy said Jacques was healthy enough to return to work, he reported back to the naval base in Toulon for duty. The romance with Simone did not end. She visited him in Toulon often. She and Jacques swam together in the sea and fell in love.

A year later, in July 1937, Jacques and Simone

were married in Paris. Sailors in crisp formal dress
made an archway of swords for the bride and groom.
The newlyweds went back south, settling just six
miles from the beach near the naval base at Toulon.
The next spring their son, Jean-Michel, was born.

On base in Toulon, Jacques was an artillery instructor. He continued his physical therapy, but it was still painful. He refused to use painkillers, and he tired easily. In the fall of 1936, an older officer named Philippe Tailliez offered him some advice: Jacques should swim in the nearby Mediterranean Sea. It would be good for his arm. Swimming would be less painful than the exercises Jacques was doing at the navy hospital.

One day after work, the two men swam in the sea beneath the cliffs. Tailliez was right.

Swimming felt good. The two became friends, regularly swimming together after work. The more Jacques swam, the stronger he became.

While Jacques exercised, Tailliez spearfished beneath the surface. Tailliez used aviator goggles for a mask, swimming fins made of saw blades encased in pieces of rubber, and a garden hose he'd twisted into a J-shaped snorkel. Sometimes he cooked his catch on the rocky beach and shared it with Jacques.

When Tailliez loaned Jacques his goggles, snorkel, and fins, it changed Jacques's life forever.

He was amazed by the sights beneath him: forests
of algae, kelp, and seaweed. Colorful fish he'd never
seen before. Starfish covering every rock. Jacques
could even make out the thin purple spines of
the sea urchins! Jacques glanced toward land,

with its bustling crowds, rumbling trolley cars, and
electric light poles. Back underwater, he glimpsed
an alien landscape twenty feet down that he'd
never known was there.

Just as he had been at the lake during summer camp, Jacques was hooked.

Tailliez introduced Jacques to his friend Frédéric Dumas, known to everyone as "Didi." Didi was an accomplished diver who could hold his breath and dive as deep as sixty-five feet. He was also an excellent spearfisher. One day, on a bet, he speared 280 pounds of fish in just two hours!

The three became inseparable, calling themselves the "Sea Musketeers." Jacques became their unofficial captain. He found ways to improve their equipment, such as protective suits to keep them warm, and weighted belts to help them dive deeper. Simone was an honorary member of the Sea Musketeers. She joined the three friends in dives, even while pregnant with Jean-Michel.

The Sea Musketeers pushed one another to the limits—to dive deeper, to hold their breath for longer. Jacques grew strong and was soon diving to depths of fifty or sixty feet on a single breath!

To most people, this would be a very dangerous undertaking. Jacques and the Sea Musketeers were training their bodies like professional athletes. But they didn't want to win competitions. They wanted to become what Jacques called "menfish."

Chapter 4
Underwater Breathing

To become a true "manfish," to see and learn more about the underwater world, Jacques needed to stay beneath the surface for longer than a single breath would allow. He once tried to breathe underwater through a gas mask that was hooked up to a tank of pure oxygen. The oxygen tank floated in an inner tube on the surface of the water.

Jacques understood that oxygen became poisonous when breathed too deep underwater. But this was the best underwater-breathing technology available at the time, so Jacques wanted to test *how* deep he could go before this change happened. After being underwater only a short time, he suffered a seizure, his lips trembling and his spine twisting backward. He dropped his weight belt then promptly fainted and floated, unconscious, to the surface.

OXYGEN TOXICITY

AS A PERSON DIVES DEEPER UNDERWATER, WATER PRESSURE ON THE BODY INCREASES. WHEN YOU DIVE TO THE BOTTOM OF THE DEEP END OF A POOL, YOUR EARS POP. THIS IS BECAUSE OF INCREASED WATER PRESSURE.

BREATHING PURE OXYGEN UNDER HIGH PRESSURE LEADS TO THE OXYGEN IN THE BLOOD BECOMING POISONOUS, OR TOXIC. A PERSON CAN EXPERIENCE CONFUSION, PROBLEMS BREATHING AND SEEING, AND, EVENTUALLY, LOSS OF CONSCIOUSNESS. THIS CONDITION IS CALLED *OXYGEN TOXICITY.*

On Jacques's second try, forty-five feet below the surface, the same thing happened.

Now Jacques knew at what depth oxygen became poisonous. But he did not want to repeat this scary experience. He decided not to breathe from an oxygen tank again.

Jacques turned his attention to creating something to protect his camera underwater. He settled on a simple fix: a glass fruit jar. First Jacques turned on the camera. Then he placed it in a bracket inside the jar and sealed the jar shut to keep the water out.

In the spring of 1938, Jacques's first underwater camera was ready to go. He tested it on the seafloor, pointing the camera up at Simone splashing on the surface. And it worked!

Now Jacques had even more reason to linger beneath the waves for as long as possible. He imagined all the beautiful things he could capture on film, if only he could stay underwater longer!

Jacques studied diving at the naval base's library.

He read about the ancient Greeks. As early as the fourth century BC, they were using *diving bells*. These devices were large enough to hold men inside them. He saw a sketch of Greek soldiers breathing underwater through hollow reeds so they could drill holes into enemy ships. He saw more recent pictures of men in diving helmets and heavy watertight suits, as well.

To Jacques, none of these inventions would do.

By the 1930s, divers were beginning to use tanks of compressed air to breathe underwater. But because of the high water pressure on the tanks, divers had to carefully control the flow of air by hand. Otherwise, the air would push forcefully out of the tanks, all at once.

What was needed, Jacques thought, was a "demand regulator"—something to control the flow of air from the tank to the diver's mouthpiece. It would let in just the right amount needed for each breath.

Jacques longed to swim like a fish, unattached to the surface of the water. He wanted to breathe as freely as he did on land without bothering to twist air-supply valves open and closed.

To achieve his dream, to become a "manfish," Jacques would have to invent something new.

Chapter 5
France at War

In September 1939, Germany invaded Poland. Two days later, France and Great Britain declared war on Germany. World War II had begun.

The Sea Musketeers were pulled apart. Tailliez was called away to another part of the country. Didi joined a unit of mule-driving soldiers in the mountains.

Jacques's naval cruiser in Toulon often performed drills, but it never left the area. German submarines were patrolling the Mediterranean, laying explosive mines all along the coast.

When a British torpedo boat got its propellers tangled in some steel cable, Jacques and five of his men dived beneath the surface. They sawed away at the cables while holding their breath.

It took hours and it was exhausting, but they freed
the propellers. This further convinced Jacques
how necessary it was to find a way for people to
breathe and move freely underwater.

Germany invaded Paris in June 1940. Days later, Germany's ally Italy declared war on France and started bombing Toulon. The French government surrendered. Germany now ruled France.

Jacques joined the French Resistance—an underground movement to resist the German occupation. He planted explosives beneath the French fleet. If the Germans tried to use these ships, the French could sink them first.

On land, Jacques put his photography hobby to good use. He wore a stolen uniform, pretended to be an Italian officer, and spent four hours in an Italian military office, taking pictures of top secret maps and documents for the resistance.

That December, the Cousteaus' second son was born. Jacques and Simone named him after their good friend Philippe Tailliez. Simone took Philippe and Jean-Michel to live in a village in the mountains, far from the action in Toulon. Jacques visited when he could, but these were trying times for the Cousteaus, and for all of France.

Chapter 6
The Aqua-Lung

In 1942, Jacques was transferred to a base in Marseille, a city in the south of France. German and Italian forces patrolled the streets and beaches. France waited nervously for the Allied Powers of Great Britain, the United States, and the Soviet Union to liberate their nation.

That spring, Jacques bought a 35-millimeter movie camera in a Marseille junk shop. With the help of a friend, he built a waterproof case for the camera out of metal, rubber, and glass.

Thirty-five-millimeter was the largest size of film at the time. If Jacques's new invention was successful, he could produce the clearest underwater images the world had ever seen.

The Sea Musketeers and the Cousteau family reunited, and Jacques got to work. He decided to make a film of his friends spearfishing.

All summer, Jacques free-dived and held his breath to get all the right shots. By October, Jacques was finally finished. He called his film *Eighteen Meters Down*.

If only Jacques could breathe underwater, he'd film for longer than a few seconds at a time.

Simone's father put Jacques in touch with an engineer from Air Liquide named Émile Gagnan. Gagnan was already working on the type of regulator Jacques needed. The two met in Paris in December of 1942 to develop the regulator for underwater use.

Their first model was no good. When Jacques

ÉMILE GAGNAN

tested it in a river outside of Paris, he had to stay perfectly flat to get the proper amount of air.

On their way back to the lab they figured out how to fix it, and their second attempt was a success!

Gagnan and Cousteau applied for a patent. They called their invention the Aqua-Lung. Eventually, it would become known as Self-Contained Underwater Breathing Apparatus, or SCUBA.

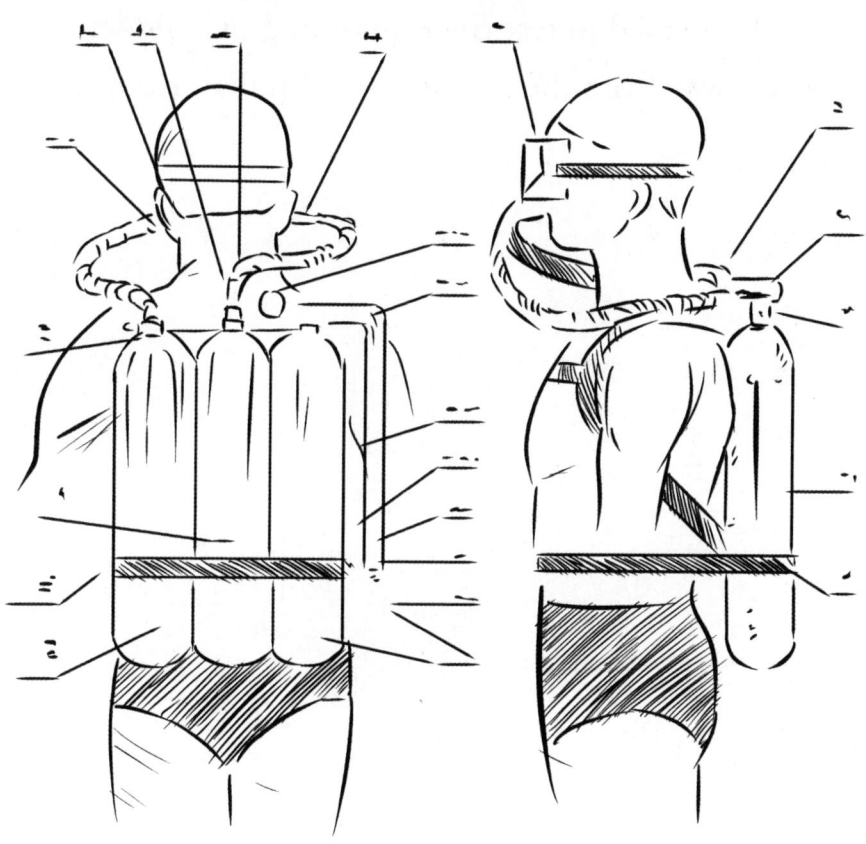

Jacques returned south. That summer, the Cousteaus and the Sea Musketeers rented a house on the beach. Jacques could hardly wait for his Aqua-Lung to arrive. In June, engineers at Air Liquide packed the world's first official Aqua-Lung into a wooden case and sent it to Jacques by train.

He decided to test the Aqua-Lung in a hidden cove, away from the prying eyes of Italian troops.

Simone put on a mask and snorkel and swam out with Jacques. She would float on the surface and watch Jacques from above. If he got into trouble Simone would signal to the shore, where Didi was ready to come to the rescue.

The moment Jacques had imagined for so
long had finally arrived. The Aqua-Lung worked
like a dream. At last, he could glide smoothly
through the water as a manfish. He did flips and
somersaults. He stood upside down, balancing
himself on one finger and laughing.
He waved up to Simone. She waved
back. And not once was his
airflow interrupted.

Feeling bold,
Jacques swam to
an underwater cave
the Sea Musketeers
had always longed
to explore. Jacques
entered the narrow
tunnel cautiously.
The roof was covered in
spiny lobsters. He grabbed
two and swam out.

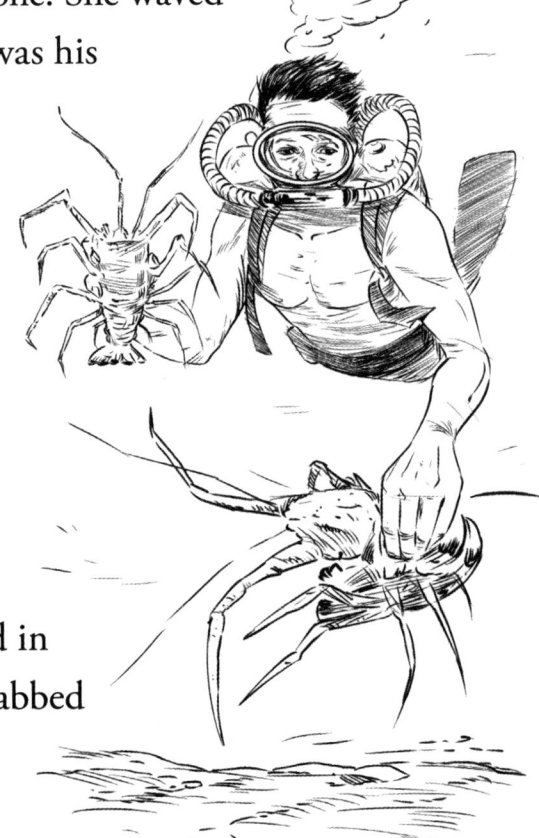

Simone dived down to meet him. Jacques handed her the lobsters before going back for more.

Simone surfaced and placed the lobsters on a rock, surprising a local fisherman. Simone asked if he could keep an eye on her catch while she dived down for more. The man dropped his pole.

Back at the beach house, everyone feasted on lobster and discussed their plans for the Aqua-Lung. Two more cases would arrive from Paris the next month. The Sea Musketeers couldn't wait to put them to use.

That summer, the trio made five hundred dives with their Aqua-Lungs. They went deeper than anyone had free-dived before. They were testing the limits of the equipment and their own bodies.

The Sea Musketeers visited shipwrecks covered in seaweed and razor-sharp mussels. Didi found the captain's quarters in one of the ships and pretended to take a bath in the tub. Jacques almost lost his mouthpiece laughing.

All the while, Jacques's camera recorded.

Jacques showed some of the footage to a
group of French Navy admirals. Right away they
placed an order for ten Aqua-Lungs of their own.

Years later, Jacques's movie *Shipwrecks* wowed audiences at the first film festival in Cannes, France—now one of the most prestigious film festivals in the world.

Chapter 7
Pushing the Limits

On June 6, 1944—known as D-Day—
Allied troops landed on the beach at Normandy
in northern France. They began pushing the
German troops out of France.

In September, more Allied troops arrived in southern France. Marseille and Toulon were freed. By the end of the year, the entire country of France was liberated, and in April 1945, the war in Europe ended for good.

Jacques now had a desk job with the navy, and Tailliez was sent away to work as a forest ranger. Jacques was not happy with this. So he convinced the navy that he and Tailliez were more useful underwater.

They formed the Undersea Research Group. Its mission was to develop better techniques for diving and underwater photography. They also would train sailors to dive.

Tailliez and Cousteau hired Didi and three additional men, including Maurice Fargues. Over the next five years, the group's offices at Toulon's harbor grew to include a machine shop, photo lab, crew quarters, research labs, and more. They also had an oceangoing dive boat and two smaller boats.

For a year, they worked to clear the coastline of underwater mines. They also filmed *Le Rubis*, a French submarine, as it test-fired torpedoes. Jacques was fearless, floating with his camera just six feet from where a torpedo sped by.

In 1946, Jacques and Didi cave-dived at the famous Fountain of Vaucluse, near Avignon, France. Every March, water surged forth from this underground cave just like a fountain, flooding the surrounding area. Jacques wanted to find out why.

But in the cold, inky water four hundred
feet below the cave's entrance, there was trouble.
Didi's suit filled with water and he spit out his
mouthpiece. Jacques grabbed hold of his friend
and almost lost the guide rope that would pull
them to safety. The two men nearly died.

It became more important than ever for Jacques to find out how deep one could dive and remain safe. Out in the Mediterranean, Jacques went down in the water, with a guide rope around his waist. He wore a weighted belt to help him go down more quickly. Small boards were tied to the rope at intervals, so Jacques could mark his progress. Jacques made it as deep as 297 feet. He dropped his weight belt and returned to the surface.

Maurice Fargues went even deeper—to 385 feet. Then suddenly the men on the boat no longer felt his telltale tugs on the line. Quickly they hauled him up. But Fargues hung limply at the 150-foot mark.

Fargues had dove too deep. It is possible for divers at such depths to forget they are in a dangerous situation, remove their breathing mouthpieces, and drown. The crew tried to revive him, but it was no use.

Jacques and his men mourned the loss of their friend and teammate. They set the absolute diving limit at three hundred feet. Anything deeper was deadly.

Chapter 8
A Life at Sea

In just a few short years, the Aqua-Lung was being sold in the United States, Canada, and Europe. Scuba diving was becoming more and more popular among adventurous people who were curious about life underwater. In 1956, *LIFE* magazine ran a seven-page feature of Jacques's photographs.

Suddenly, Jacques Cousteau was a celebrity!

He wanted a bigger boat. The French Navy said he would have to buy it himself. But Jacques didn't have the money! Luckily, in 1950, a wealthy British politician and businessman gave Jacques enough money to buy the *Calypso*, a 140-foot-long ferryboat. The *Calypso* was seaworthy, but it would need to be renovated.

So the Cousteaus sold their house. Jacques and Simone called friends and family to raise more money. Simone sold her jewelry. The Cousteaus moved onto the ship. Their dream of an exciting life at sea was becoming a reality!

The *Calypso* was turned into a research vessel. It had an observation deck on top, and an underwater observation chamber below. The steel bubble beneath the ship had eight viewing windows and a mattress. It was just big enough for a man to lie flat on his stomach. It was perfect for filming.

The remodeled *Calypso* had space for cargo, fuel, water, a machine shop, and cold storage for food and scientific samples. It even had a wine cellar.

Jacques took a three-year leave from the navy. He wanted to spend as much time exploring the sea as possible. He assembled a crew of about twenty people: sailors, scientists, filmmakers, and, of course, Didi. Tailliez stayed in Toulon to run the Undersea Research Group. Simone joined her husband, while their sons Jean-Michel and Philippe attended boarding school. The boys would meet up with the *Calypso* on their vacations.

On November 24, 1951, the *Calypso* embarked on its first expedition. It was to the Red Sea, an inlet in the Indian Ocean between Africa and Asia. Jacques jokingly called it "a nice hot bathtub full of sharks." The night before they left, Jacques proposed a toast to his assembled crew: "*Il faut aller voir.*" (You say it like this: eel fo ALL-ay vwar.)

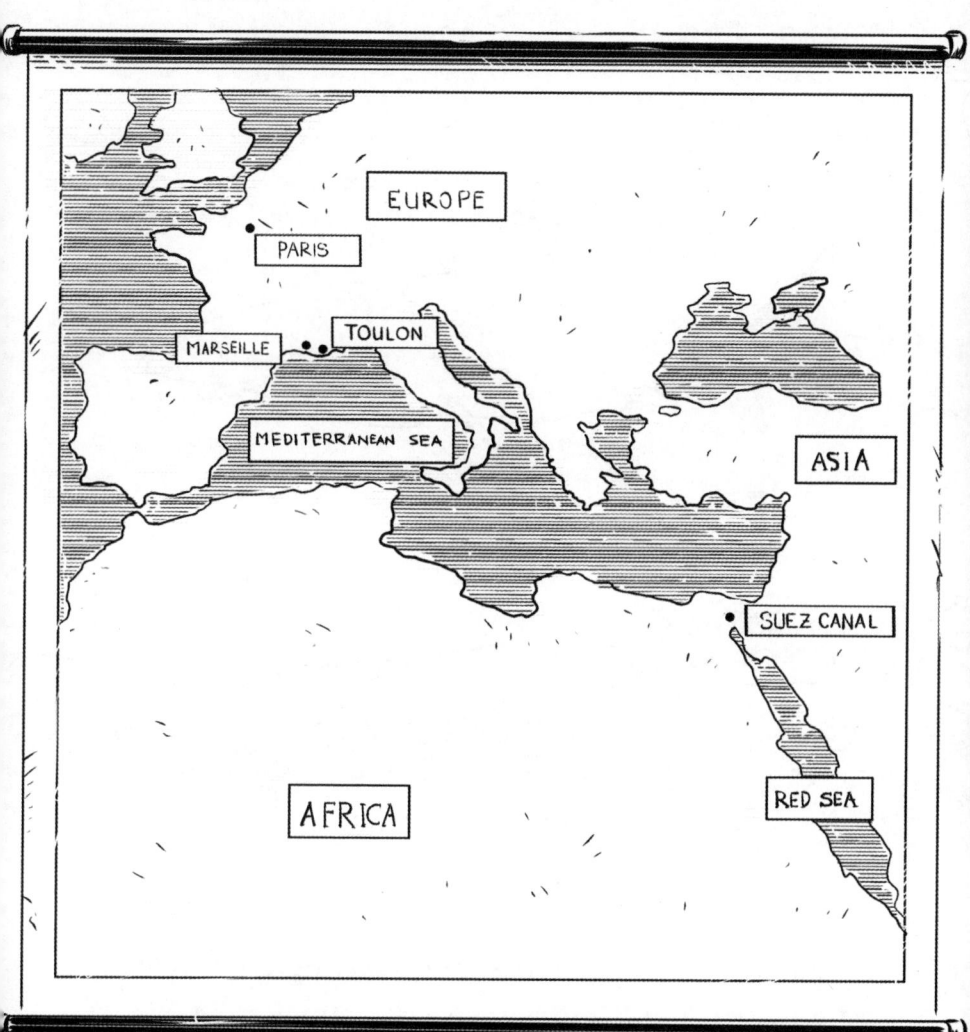

That meant, *We must go and see for ourselves.*

The entire monthlong journey was recorded.

Jacques filmed sharks and dazzling coral reefs. New species of sea creatures were discovered. New areas along the seabed were identified as containing oil. Water samples were collected at various depths and studied by scientists on board.

The expedition was a resounding success, the first of many.

In 1952, the *Calypso* excavated a Greek shipwreck more than two thousand years old off the coast of Marseille. Jacques established the French Office of Undersea Technology in Toulon to invent and improve upon undersea equipment and technologies.

In 1953, Jacques's first book was published. Written with Didi, *The Silent World* described the development of the Aqua-Lung, and the Undersea Research Group's many adventures.

It was a *New York Times* Best Seller, with nearly half a million copies sold by the end of the year. Eventually, the book would be translated into more than twenty languages and sell more than five million copies.

THE SILENT WORLD

by CAPTAIN J.Y. COUSTEAU with *Frédéric Dumas*

In 1954, an oil company paid Jacques to explore the Persian Gulf for oil deposits. Chiseling rock 150 feet below the surface was hard work. The crew also had to watch out for schools of poisonous sea snakes. It was not the kind of work Jacques wanted to do, but he needed the money to pay the *Calypso*'s bills.

Jacques wanted to film the first full-length underwater color movie. He invested in new lighting equipment and cameras. He hired a codirector, and transformed the *Calypso* into a floating movie studio.

The now-familiar trip across the Mediterranean was one big party. On their way to the Red Sea, the crew played cards, sunbathed on the deck, and enjoyed long dinners filled with conversation and many bottles of wine. There was even a dog on board, a dachshund named Bulle.

Jacques's film was also called *The Silent World*.
It came out in 1956. Audiences were astounded.
They gasped as hundreds of porpoises leaped in
the air like aquatic acrobats. They laughed at Jo Jo,
a large *mérou* fish. Jo Jo got so used to being fed
scraps, the fish had to be locked in a shark cage so it
wouldn't follow the divers everywhere they swam.
And people cried as a school of hungry sharks tore
a baby whale to pieces in a bloody feeding frenzy.

In France, the film won the Palme d'Or,
the grand prize at the Cannes Film Festival.
In the United States, it won the Academy Award
for Best Documentary.

With *The Silent World*, Jacques succeeded in
capturing the imagination of the *entire* world.

Chapter 9
A Life Under the Sea

In 1957, Prince Rainier III
of Monaco (a tiny country
on the southern coast of
France) offered Jacques
a job: Would he like
to be director of the
Oceanographic
Museum of Monaco?
Jacques could
continue his work
on the *Calypso*.
Jacques accepted and

PRINCE RAINIER III

retired from the navy. He stocked the museum's
aquariums with exotic creatures he brought back
from his expeditions.

OCEANOGRAPHIC MUSEUM OF MONACO

The more Jacques studied the oceans,
the more he realized how fragile they were.
European nations kept dumping garbage into the
Mediterranean Sea. The coastal ecosystem—or
living environment—that Jacques had explored
barely twenty years ago was dying.

Jacques also dreamed of a day when humans
could live underwater. He thought people would

one day live on the continental shelf. That is the edge of a continent that lies underwater before sloping down to the ocean floor. Jacques conducted three experiments—Conshelf I, II, and III—to see just what life underwater could be like.

In the Conshelf I experiment of 1962, two "aquanauts," as Jacques called them, lived thirty-seven feet below the surface. Their "home" was a watertight capsule the size of a large bedroom. Air was pumped in from the surface. Unlike sailors on a submarine, the aquanauts could come and go through a hole in the floor of the chamber called a *moon pool*.

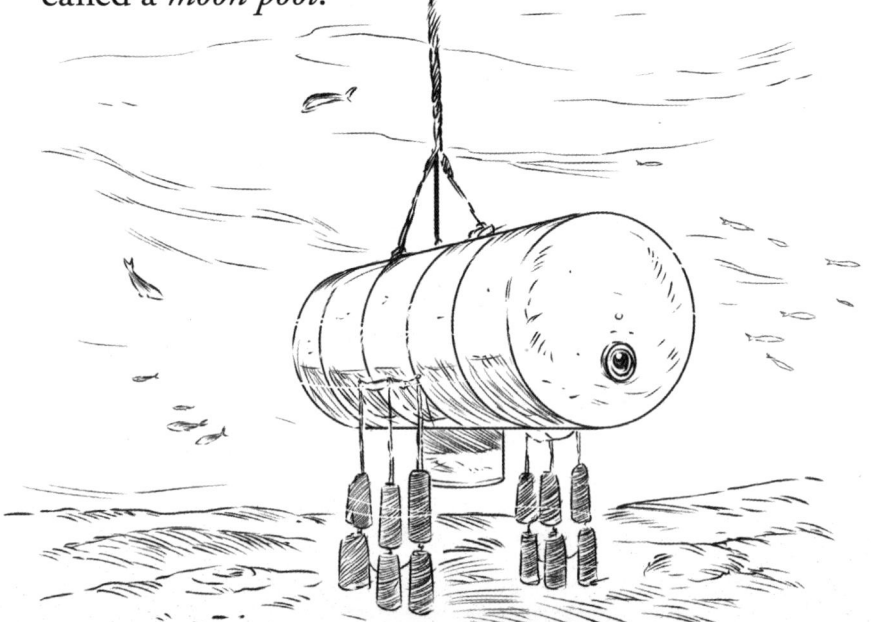

Air pressure from inside the room prevented the water from flooding the capsule.

For one week, they lived and worked underwater off the coast of Marseille. They dived as deep as eighty feet but never rose higher than their "home."

They breathed a mixture of 80 percent oxygen and 20 percent nitrogen, the opposite of what they'd breathe on dry land. Doctors visited daily to check on them. Jacques dived, too, sometimes with journalists. When the aquanauts returned to the surface at the end of the week, they were in excellent health.

Jacques had proven to the world that men could live and work underwater. He predicted that by the year 2000, "water people" would be born in underwater homes. They would undergo surgery to implant gills in their necks, and swim up to a mile deep. Fellow scientists called this science fiction. But science fiction, Jacques said, often foretold of future realities.

The next year, Conshelf II took place in the Red Sea off the coast of Sudan. They were by a coral reef. This time, two underwater capsules were used.

Five people—and a pet parrot—lived thirty-three feet below the surface in the Starfish House for a full month. The Starfish House was much larger than the bedroom-size capsule used in Conshelf I. There were five rooms,

including a full kitchen with viewing portholes.
The cook even trained a triggerfish to come into
the moon pool for a treat when he tapped on
the glass.

JULES VERNE (1828–1905)

FRENCH NOVELIST JULES VERNE IS KNOWN
AS THE "FATHER OF SCIENCE FICTION." MUCH OF
THE TECHNOLOGY HE DREAMED UP IN HIS BOOKS
BECAME REALITY AFTER HIS DEATH.

VERNE DESCRIBED A SPACESHIP-LIKE ROCKET
IN HIS BOOK *FROM THE EARTH TO THE MOON*,
MORE THAN A CENTURY BEFORE NEIL ARMSTRONG'S
FAMOUS VOYAGE. THE ELECTRIC-POWERED
SUBMARINE IN *TWENTY THOUSAND LEAGUES UNDER
THE SEA* WAS JUST A FANTASY IN 1869, AS WAS A
WEAPON THAT WORKED LIKE A MODERN TASER GUN.

TODAY, JULES VERNE IS THE SECOND MOST-
TRANSLATED AUTHOR IN THE WORLD.

One day, Simone dived down to Starfish House to cook the crew dinner. She loved the experience. There was wine, air-conditioning, music, television, and good company! At night, the reef outside glowed! This was because of bioluminescence, a chemical reaction that creates light energy.

Simone returned with Jacques one night to celebrate their twenty-sixth wedding anniversary. They toasted with flat champagne. Because of the pressurized air, there were no bubbles.

A second habitat called Deep Cabin sat eighty-two feet deep. Two aquanauts lived there for a week. They conducted experiments at depths of up to four hundred feet. Deep Cabin was miserably hot, and there were minor leaks—but the men were fine. They breathed a mixture of

helium and oxygen, which made their voices comically high.

The Conshelf II project was made into a movie. *World Without Sun* opened in December of 1964, and once again, Jacques won the Oscar for Best Documentary.

Jacques had proven men could live in depths up to one hundred feet, and work even deeper. This was important news for oil companies. The age of underwater oil drilling had begun. Big companies wanted to know how much farther down men could work.

So in 1965, Conshelf III put six men—including Jacques's twenty-four-year-old son Philippe—into a globe-shaped habitat off the coast of Nice, France.

For three weeks, they lived and worked more than three hundred feet beneath the surface. They worked on a mock-up oil well. This was to see if people could do hard physical jobs underwater. Breathing air that was 98 percent helium dulled their senses of taste and smell. And their voices were so high, conversation was all but impossible. But the experiment was a success.

Life aboard Conshelf III was also filmed, but it wasn't made into a movie.

Jacques Cousteau was coming to television.

Chapter 10
Television Star

In 1960, there were more than fifty million TV sets in America alone. Jacques had been successful with books and movies, but he wanted to inspire the world with the beauty of the oceans. Television was the way to go.

In April of 1966, CBS aired a one-hour special on Conshelf III. Narrated by movie star Orson Welles, it reached millions.

Soon after, rival network ABC offered Jacques $4.2 million to produce twelve hour-long television shows. He jumped at the opportunity.

After more than fifteen years of constant use, the *Calypso* had seen a lot of wear and tear. Jacques set about renovating it. Space was made for two "Sea Fleas." These were one-man submarines that could dive as deep as one thousand feet to shoot from just the right angle. New scuba suits were bought.

The Undersea World of Jacques Cousteau aired four times a year for three years. It was later renewed for twenty-four additional episodes. The crew of the *Calypso* would be filming at sea for years. Philippe Cousteau joined the crew. His brother Jean-Michel made the arrangements for the many international trips.

In 1967, the *Calypso* set sail from Monaco. Hundreds of onlookers released confetti and balloons from the cliffs surrounding the harbor.

The first episode, "Sharks," premiered in 1968 to rave reviews. People were amazed to see one of Cousteau's divers riding a sixty-foot whale shark!

Over the years, the crew filmed sea otters
in Alaska, manatees in Florida, and twenty
million squid off the coast of California. They
studied marine iguanas on the Galápagos Islands
and "adopted" two fur seals in South Africa.
They were named Cristobal and Pepito. Jacques
and his crew searched for buried treasure in the
Caribbean, and for Inca gold in the depths of
Lake Titicaca on the border of Peru and Bolivia.

THE SIX-DAY WAR

IN JUNE OF 1967, ISRAEL AND ITS ARAB NEIGHBORS WERE AT WAR. THE FIGHTING LASTED FOR SIX DAYS. BY JUNE 10, ISRAEL HAD CAPTURED THE SINAI PENINSULA FROM EGYPT. NOW ISRAEL CONTROLLED THE EAST SIDE OF THE RED SEA, AND EGYPT CONTROLLED THE WEST.

WHILE FILMING IN THE RED SEA, THE *CALYPSO* WAS CAUGHT IN THE CROSS FIRE BETWEEN EGYPT AND ISRAEL. AN ISRAELI FIGHTER JET EVEN FIRED ON THE SHIP BY ACCIDENT! THE CREW, SLEEPING BELOWDECKS, WAS TERRIFIED.

OVER THE NEXT TWO MONTHS, EGYPTIAN AUTHORITIES BOARDED THE *CALYPSO* MULTIPLE TIMES TO INSPECT IT, MAKING EVERYONE ANXIOUS. THE *CALYPSO* WAS NOT ALLOWED TO DOCK ON EGYPTIAN SHORES. EVEN WORSE, EGYPT HAD SUNK A NUMBER OF SHIPS TO BLOCK ACCESS TO THE SUEZ CANAL, WHICH CONNECTED THE RED SEA TO THE MEDITERRANEAN. THE CANAL WOULD NOT REOPEN UNTIL 1975.

THE *CALYPSO* WAS STUCK. FINALLY, JACQUES AND THE *CALYPSO* CREW LEFT THE AREA BY TAKING A DIFFERENT ROUTE, SOUTH AND AROUND THE HORN OF AFRICA.

IN 1979, EGYPT AND ISRAEL SIGNED A PEACE
TREATY, AND ISRAEL HANDED THE SINAI PENINSULA
BACK TO EGYPT.

The Undersea World of Jacques Cousteau
brought the beauty of the underwater world into
American living rooms. And it was a hit! The
Calypso crew was handsome and daring. Viewers
loved their captain, Jacques Cousteau, with his
heavy French accent and famous red wool cap.
The show ran for eight years, until 1976.

Chapter 11
Future Generations

Jacques loved making movies. But for him, they were a way to raise awareness about the fragile state of our beautiful planet. In the sixties and seventies, the world's rivers, lakes, and oceans had become a dumping ground for sewage, garbage, and nuclear waste. Jacques spoke of his beloved Mediterranean Sea, fearing it "would be the first to die."

In 1973, he established the Cousteau Society to help protect the world's oceans. Jacques was chairman; his son Philippe was vice president. They  testified before the United States Congress and other government groups about reducing pollution.

By the end of the year, more than 120,000 people had donated money to the Cousteau Society. Four years later, that number doubled.

Jacques traveled the world giving lectures and raising money for the society. In 1977, he received an environmental prize from the United Nations for his work.

Jacques Cousteau had once said that when a person is lucky enough to be given an interesting life, that person had a duty to share it with the world. But while Jacques was travelling and sharing his passion with the world, he received some terrible news. In June 1979, while attempting to land his seaplane on the Tagus River in Portugal, Philippe Cousteau crashed. The plane exploded into pieces. Philippe's body was not found for three days. Jacques waited anxiously with Simone and Jean-Michel. Finally, they got the news they'd been dreading. Philippe was dead. His family buried him at sea, twenty-five miles off the coast of Portugal.

Jean-Michel took over Philippe's duties at the Cousteau Society.

Jacques was overcome with grief. He never spoke publicly about his beloved son Philippe again.

How did he cope with this terrible sadness? He threw himself into his work, exploring the Amazon and Mississippi Rivers as well as re-creating the routes of famous explorers.

For Simone, the loss of her son was equally great. She retreated to her cabin on the *Calypso*. In 1990, she died of cancer.

The year after Simone's death, Jacques married Francine Triplet, whom he had known for fifteen years.

By the early 1990s, Jacques was in his eighties. But was he was ready to retire? Not at all! Oil companies and nations around the world were trying to mine the continent of Antarctica for its minerals and oil. To Jacques, this was unacceptable.

He met with world leaders. He collected more than a million signatures from ordinary people. "May this continent," he said, "the last explored by humankind, be the first one to be spared by humankind."

And naturally, Jacques made a movie about it. With six children from different countries around the world, he journeyed to the continent. As if on cue, they were greeted in Antarctica by four humpback whales. Jacques and the children even built an igloo.

Copies of the film were sent to every member of the US Congress and the Supreme Court. Jacques's efforts worked. Antarctica was closed to private development. The land could be used only for scientific research.

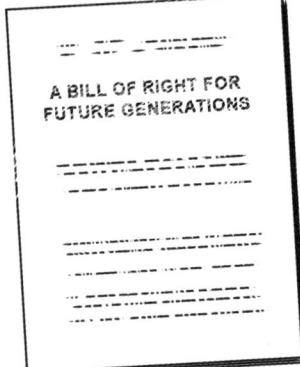

In 1991, Jacques asked the United Nations to adopt a Bill of Rights for Future Generations. He wanted the world to know that if present-day problems of pollution were not fixed soon, its children and grandchildren would suffer. Millions of signatures were collected by the Cousteau Society and other organizations. Jacques believed that "future generations have a right to an uncontaminated and undamaged Earth."

In 1997, the wording of the Bill of Rights was approved by the UN General Conference.

That same year, Jacques suffered a heart attack, and on June 25—two weeks after his eighty-seventh birthday—he passed away in his Paris apartment.

In 2001, five children from around the world read his Bill of Rights aloud to the United Nations.

A single French volunteer—no doubt inspired by the great Jacques Cousteau—had delivered the final six thousand signatures required for its passage.

In the larger sense, Jacques Cousteau's work will never truly be finished. But it is continued by those he left behind. His second wife, Francine, became head of the Cousteau Society. His first son, Jean-Michel, wrote a book about Jacques and makes documentary films.

In 2014, more than fifty years after the Conshelf experiments, Jacques's grandson, Fabien, lived underwater for one month at a depth of sixty feet.

He was studying the effects of climate change and pollution on the coral reefs off the Florida Keys.

Jacques had two children with Francine—Diane and Pierre-Yves. Pierre is CEO of Cousteau Divers, a branch of the Cousteau Society dedicated to uniting the world's divers to protect marine life.

In 1996, Jacques's beloved *Calypso* was struck by a barge in Singapore and sank in the harbor. It was quickly recovered and transported to France. The Cousteau Society hopes to repair it so the *Calypso* can inspire a whole new generation to love and protect the world's oceans.

TIMELINE OF
JACQUES COUSTEAU'S LIFE

1910 — Born on June 11 in Saint-André-de-Cubzac, France

1914 — Learns to swim at seaside resort of Deauville

1920 — Moves to New York City; attends summer camp in Vermont

1923 — Moves back to France; purchases first movie camera

1930 — Joins the French Navy

1936 — Crashes his father's sports car in the Vosges Mountains
Dives underwater using goggles for the first time

1937 — Marries Simone Melchior

1943 — Tests the world's first Aqua-Lung in the waters off Sanary

1945 — Forms the Undersea Research Group

1950 — Buys the *Calypso*

1953 — Publishes first book, *The Silent World*, with Frédéric Dumas

1956 — *The Silent World* movie premieres, astounding audiences

1957 — Becomes director of the Oceanographic Museum of Monaco
Retires from the navy

1962–1965 — Conshelf I, II, and III experiments

1968 — *The Undersea World of Jacques Cousteau* premieres

1973 — Establishes the Cousteau Society

1979 — Philippe Cousteau, Jacques's youngest son, dies in Portugal

1985 — Receives the Presidential Medal of Freedom
from Ronald Reagan

1990 — Wife, Simone, dies of cancer

1991 — Marries second wife, Francine Triplet

1996 — *Calypso* sinks in Singapore Harbor

1997 — Dies in Paris

TIMELINE OF THE WORLD

Boy Scouts of America is founded	1910
The *Titanic* sinks on April 15	1912
World War I begins	1914
World War I ends; Spanish influenza breaks out in Europe, infecting half a billion worldwide over the next two years	1918
The Band-Aid is invented	1920
Penicillin is discovered by Alexander Fleming	1928
The Empire State Building opens in New York City	1931
Amelia Earhart, the first woman to fly solo across the Atlantic, vanishes	1937
Germany invades Poland; World War II begins	1939
United States drops atomic bombs on Hiroshima and Nagasaki; World War II ends	1945
The nation of Israel is founded	1948
Elvis Presley's song "Hound Dog" hits the top of the charts	1956
Six-Day War is fought between Israel and Egypt, Syria, and Jordan	1967
Walt Disney World opens in Florida	1971
George Lucas's movie *Star Wars* opens	1977
The Motorola DynaTAC 8000X, the world's first cell phone, goes on sale. It weighs nearly two pounds and costs $3,995.	1984
Nelson Mandela is freed from prison in South Africa after twenty-seven years	1990
Diana, Princess of Wales, is killed in a car crash in Paris	1997

BIBLIOGRAPHY

Cousteau, Jacques, and Frédéric Dumas. **The Silent World.** Harper & Brothers Publishers: New York, 1953.

Cousteau, Jean-Michel, with Daniel Paisner. **My Father, the Captain: My Life with Jacques Cousteau.** National Geographic Society: Washington, 2010.

* DuTemple, Lesley A. **Jacques Cousteau.** Learner Publications Company: Minneapolis, 2000.

Jonas, Gerald. **"Jacques Cousteau, Oceans' Impresario, Dies."** *The New York Times,* June 26, 1997.

Matsen, Brad. **Jacques Cousteau: The Sea King.** Pantheon Books: New York, 2009.

* Ollhoff, Jim. **Jacques Cousteau.** ABDO Publishing Company: Minneapolis, 2014.

* Yaccarino, Dan. **The Fantastic Undersea Life of Jacques Cousteau.** Alfred A. Knopf: New York, 2009.

* Books for young readers